This book is dedicated to all who cherish America's history as a vast heritage of people and events—some heroic, some inglorious, but all part of America's epic struggle to come of age—and to all who know that understanding the past is essential to dealing with the present.

FORT CLATSOP
THE STORY BEHIND THE SCENERY®

by Daniel J. Dattilio

Daniel J. Dattilio, a National Park Service career employee, has a liberal arts degree with emphasis on history and education. Dan was an interpreter at both Jefferson National Expansion Memorial in St. Louis, Missouri—the beginning of the Lewis and Clark Trail— and at Fort Clatsop National Memorial at Astoria, Oregon—the end of the Trail.

Fort Clatsop National Memorial, *located in the northwest corner of Oregon, was set aside in 1958 to preserve the site of Lewis and Clark's 1805-06 winter camp.*

Front cover: Fort Clatsop, photo by Andrew Cier. Inside front cover: Fort construction, photo by Craig Harmel. Page 1: At the Pacific's edge, photo by Craig Harmel.

Edited by Russell D. Butcher. Book design by K. C. DenDooven.

Fourth Printing, 2000

FORT CLATSOP: THE STORY BEHIND THE SCENERY. © 1986 KC PUBLICATIONS, INC.
"The Story Behind the Scenery"; "in pictures... The Continuing Story"; the parallelogram forms and colors within are registered in the U.S. Patent and Trademark Office.
LC 86-81743. ISBN 0-88714-011-4.

December 8th 1805

We having fixed on this situation as the one best Calculated
for our Winter quarters, my
principal object is to look out a
place to make Salt, blaze the
rout that they men out hunting might find the direction to
the fort, and see the probability
of game in that direction.

Prologue

"Of courage undaunted; possessing a firmness and perseverance of purpose which nothing but impossibilities could divert from its direction; careful as a father of those committed to his charge, yet steady in the maintenance of order and discipline; intimate with Indian character, customs, and principals; habituated to the hunting life; guarded by exact observation of the vegetables and animals of his own country, against losing time in the description of objects already possessed; honest, disinterested, liberal, of sound understanding, and a fidelity to truth so scrupulous that whatever he should report would be as certain as if seen by ourselves—with all these qualifications, as if selected and implanted by nature in one body for this express purpose. I could have no hesitation in confiding the enterprise to him."

—President Thomas Jefferson's reference to Meriwether Lewis's command of the Corps of Volunteers for Northwest Discovery

Lewis and Clark's success in reaching the Pacific Ocean was significant in several ways, but of most importance was the accomplishment of their principal goal as directed by President Thomas Jefferson. Yet in many ways, one of their greatest challenges still lay ahead. The members of the Corps of Discovery first heard the roar of the Pacific as they tried to find comfort in their rotting buckskin clothing that scarcely held together. The weather was often extremely depressing, their health poor, and food and fresh water scarce. For the civilized world to learn what the Lewis and Clark Expedition had accomplished, these intrepid explorers, amid miserable conditions, would have to recover and prepare, and once again challenge and conquer 4,000 miles of hostile wilderness.

Under the courageous leadership of Meriwether Lewis and William Clark, the challenge to succeed against the odds was squarely met. A small protective fortification was built; skillful hunters provided sufficient food and skins for clothes; and Lewis and Clark filled their journals with the wonder of the land that would turn the eyes of the United States to the West. A mere six months after leaving the Pacific coast, Lewis and Clark achieved a triumphant return to St. Louis. The nation would forever remember that in 1805, Fort Clatsop, the westernmost outpost of the United States, was hewn out of the wilderness. Thus was blazed the trail that would lead to the expansion and growth of a new world power.

November 24th, Sunday, 1805

"added to the . . . advantages in being near the Sea Coast one most Strikeing one occurs to me i.e, the Climate which must be from every appearance much milder than that above the 1st range of Mountains. The Indians are Slightly Clothed and give an account of but little Snow, and the weather which we have experienced since we arrived in the neighbourhood of the Sea coast has been verr warm. . . . If this Should be the case it will most Certainly be the best Situation of our Naked party dressed as they are altogether in leather.

William Clark

Preceding Pages: Chief among the accomplishments at Fort Clatsop were the scientific notations and maps compiled by Lewis and Clark. But also important were the journals, which contained the impressions, feelings, and concerns of ordinary men who had done extraordinary things. Photo by Craig Harmel.

4

To the Pacific

The Lewis and Clark Expedition of 1804–06 was the first major exploration officially promoted and financed by the United States government. At the cost of $2,500 in congressionally approved funds—a substantial sum in those days—the expedition proved to be one of the most successful ever undertaken. It was the fulfillment of President Thomas Jefferson's long-held dream of extending the influence of the United States across the continent and challenging British expansion into the Pacific Northwest, where control of the lucrative fur trade was of great importance.

The expedition covered more than 8,000 miles on foot, by boat, by canoe, and on horseback from the mouth of the Missouri River to the mouth of the Columbia River and back. The courageous group traveled through a vast uncharted wilderness inhabited by grizzly bears, rattlesnakes, and a multitude of Indian tribes. Even though they encountered dozens of dangers along the wild rivers and over the rugged mountains, only a single man perished and two deserted.

The expedition returned with more than a million words of written information about the flora and fauna, geography, weather, and ethnology of the West. The fruits of this monumental adventure shaped the political and economic future of the North American continent.

Meriwether Lewis and William Clark were members of the U.S. Regular Army, and Lewis was the President's personal secretary. Although Clark was officially recruited as a second lieutenant, Lewis unofficially promoted him to captain as far as he and the expedition were concerned. The rank and file was selected with great care. Lewis insisted that the volunteers be "good hunters; stout, healthy, unmarried men, accustomed to the woods, and capable of bearing bodily fa-

ANDREW CIER

The explorers' feelings of jubilation upon reaching the Pacific Ocean were soon replaced with depressing thoughts. On the tempestuous Oregon coast, violent ocean storms battered the party as they experienced a shortage of food and fresh water. Many members became seasick, having no place to sleep other than their canoes, which rolled constantly in the ocean surf. Along with the explorers, Sacagawea endured these hardships. But for her there was an additional worry—the well-being of her infant son.

Conditions grew worse as the party remained on the north side of the Columbia River. ". . . all wet and disagreeable" wrote Clark, "a bad place to camp all around this great bend is high land thickly timbered brushey & almost impossible to penetrate." Many of the men expressed a desire "to winter near the falls" of the Cascade Mountains.

tigues to a considerable degree." Many of the recruits were seasoned soldiers from frontier forts throughout the Ohio Valley. Additionally there were interpreters; "French water-men"; Clark's slave, York; and Lewis's Newfoundland dog, Seaman.

On May 14, 1804, 45 men ventured forth against the Missouri's powerful current in a 55-foot keelboat and two smaller canoelike crafts called pirogues. After a difficult five-month journey, they spent their first winter at Fort Mandan in present-day North Dakota. Captains Lewis and Clark hired a French fur trader, Toussaint Charbonneau, as an interpreter and thereby also gained the vital services of his Shoshone Indian wife, Sacagawea. Since no woman ever accompanied a war party, she confirmed the expedition's friendly intentions to all the Indian tribes they encountered.

A few of the explorers were dispatched back to St. Louis in the spring of 1805 with floral and faunal specimens and reports to be delivered to the President. Meanwhile the permanent party, now numbering 33 persons, continued upriver. When the boats and canoes scraped the bottom of the Missouri's headwaters, Sacagawea assisted in the purchase of horses from her tribe for the formidable crossing of the Rocky Mountains—notably the steep, rugged, and snowy Bitterroots of northern Idaho, where the party suffered from cold, hunger, and exhaustion.

In late September, the explorers came to the Clearwater River—a wild, rapids-filled tributary in the Columbia River watershed of the Pacific Northwest. Captain Lewis commented upon "the flattering prospect of the final success of the expedition," now that they had finally left behind the United States' recently purchased Louisiana Territory and were now in the disputed Oregon Country. Even though nearly all the men were ill, they succeeded in building five large dugout canoes in which they would complete their westward journey to the Pacific Ocean.

CRAIG HARMEL

"A Mountain which we Suppose to be Mt. Hood, S. 85° E about 47 miles distance from the mouth of quick sand river [Sandy]. This Mtⁿ is covered with Snow and in the range of mountains which we have passed through and is of a conical form but rugid."

WILLIAM CLARK.
NOVEMBER 3, 1805

On October 31, after portaging around the last major obstacle, the Cascades of the Columbia, the explorers were thrilled to see that the river was now wide and smooth and with "everry appearance of being effected by the tide."* They also passed from the arid, treeless plains east of the Cascade Range to the lush, green, heavily forested country west of the volcano-crowned mountains. Along the river banks they saw huge trees, unlike any they had seen before, some towering more than 200 feet. They correctly identified Mount Hood to the south and Mount St. Helens to the north, magnificent dome-shaped volcanic peaks that had been discovered during the 1792 sea exploration of British Captain George Vancouver. The men were now spurred on by the knowledge that their goal was near, and they raced their canoes forward, averaging some 30 miles per day.

Then, on November 7, 1805, William Clark proclaimed, "Ocian in view! O! the joy." But the broad estuary of the Columbia had deceived Captain Clark. While the explorers were still a few miles from an unobstructed ocean view, "the roreing

---

*Spellings are printed as they appeared in the Expedition's journals.

DAVID MUENCH

". . . we found Some drift pine . . . of which we made fires."

WILLIAM CLARK

From atop Cape Disappointment the party viewed the great Pacific Ocean which they had been ". . . so long anxious to See." At the base of this rocky prominence Clark remarked, "the waves appear to brake with tremendious force in every direction. . ." They hoped to make contact with a trading vessel at the mouth of the Columbia River and obtain trinkets for trade with the Indians on their long return journey in the spring.

or noise made by the waves braking on the rockey Shores" proved they were nearly there.

Upon reaching their long-anticipated goal, the canoeists were immediately confronted by new difficulties at the turbulent mouth of the great river. As they sought refuge in a bay along the north shore, floating logs up to seven feet in diameter threatened to crush their craft; and steep hills bordering the river left no level ground on which to camp. Consequently, they were forced to spend the first night, at the end of their year-and-a-half westward trek, upon logs that rolled about in the ocean surf. Many members became seasick. To make matters worse, there was no fresh water and "nothing to eate but dried fish," and the continual rain made "every man as wet

as water could make them." Despite these disagreeable circumstances, Clark noted that "they are chearfull and anxious to See further into the Ocian."

After enduring five days of this misery, three men set out by canoe and soon discovered a good sandy beach just a short distance to the west, at or near present Fort Columbia, Washington. Once the explorers had moved to this better location, Clark and 11 other men set out on foot "to see more of the main *Ocian*" from the hook-shaped peninsula at the Columbia's mouth. This area had been visited by British Captain John Meares in 1788. Failing to find a river that earlier reports indicated might be there, Meares named this promontory Cape Disappointment. On their excursion one member of the group shot and killed a "Buzzard" that we know, from the nearly ten-foot wingspan, had to have been a California condor, an endangered species that was last recorded in Oregon in 1913.

Clark reported that, upon reaching the promontory, his men beheld "with estonishment the high waves dashing against the rocks & this emence Ocian." Facing into near-constant wind, from atop the open, grassy exposure to the southwest, Clark and party could see the mighty Columbia River and Pacific Ocean. Below them the sea unleashed its fury as waves broke against the steep, high basalt cliffs inhabited only by sparse vegetation and shore birds. In the Columbia's mouth could be seen shallow, treacherous sandbars that would claim many ships. On the south shore Clark observed that Point Adams, also named by a British sea captain, would be nearly covered at high tide. From there a sandy beach stretched south some 15 miles to Tillamook Head, rising majestically more than a thousand feet above the Pacific shore.

For several days the expedition's members were plagued by stormy weather that brought torrential rains and gale-force winds—so typical of November along the Pacific Northwest coast. "O! how horriable is the day," wrote Clark.

Compounding their problems was the difficulty of obtaining food. The local Chinook Indians not only had little food for trade, but the tribe also demanded more in trade for what they did have than the explorers could afford. As if this were not enough, the men now discovered that their clothing had begun to mildew and rot from the nearly continuous rainfall and penetrating humidity.

In the midst of these miseries, the men debated where they should spend the winter. While some favored heading back toward the Cascades to drier country, a majority voted in favor of a site across the river. This decision was strongly influenced by the Indians who reported that elk were more plentiful along the opposite shore, while the smaller deer predominated upriver. There were also convenient places across the river for boiling seawater to obtain salt—an important commodity that the expedition had long ago run out of on the westward journey.

Lewis and Clark concluded that it was more important to have ready access to salt and to rely upon the elk, since they were "easier to kill, & better meat (in the Winter when pore) and Skins better for the Clothes of our party . . ." [easier to hunt, had better meat, and provided ample skins

for clothes]. Another inducement for remaining near the Pacific shore was the chance of meeting a trading vessel. With a letter of credit signed by President Jefferson, the weary explorers hoped to "precure a fresh Supply of Indian trinkets to purchase provisions on our return home . . ."

As the explorers attempted to cross the river's wide mouth on November 25, high rolling swells threatened to capsize their bulky dugouts. No sooner had they decided to make the crossing further upstream, where the river was narrower and more sheltered from the sea, than some Clatsop Indians, a subgroup of the Chinook tribe who had recently been accompanying the explorers,

The explorers were enthralled with the immensity of the Pacific Ocean and the force with which waves broke against the rocks.

suddenly set out and "crossed the river through emence high waves." Clark referred to the Clatsops as "certainly the best Canoe navigaters I ever saw." On the following day, the expedition traveled several miles upriver and crossed over to what is now the Oregon shore.

Conditions did not improve on the Columbia's south bank. Rain continued making all "wet and disagreeable," rotting clothing and tents. Dry wood could not be found or bartered for, the hunters discovered that the forest was virtually impenetrable, waterfowl were too elusive to shoot, and the Clatsops demanded as much in trade for their goods as had the Chinooks. "O! how dis-

agreeable is our Situation dureing this dreadful weather," Clark lamented.

Nevertheless, Clark continued to record interesting observations in his journal. Although harassed by terrible weather and lack of food, he found time to describe a nearby beach "formed of butiful pebble of various colours." He recorded several species of birds, trees, plants, and insects and carefully depicted the Chinookan style of burial. On December 1, he wittily noted that it had been 24 days since their arrival in "Sight of the Great Western Ocian," explaining that he could not call it the Pacific Ocean, for "I have not Seen one pacific day Since my arrival in its vicinity."

The Fort

On November 29, Lewis and five men set out in a "small Indian canoe . . . calculated to ride the waves," and found "a good situation and Elk sufficent to winter on." As soon as the weather permitted, the explorers left their brief encampment on what is now called Tongue Point and proceeded around a prominent peninsula where the city of Astoria is now situated. They paddled a few miles up a small river called the Netul by the Indians, but subsequently renamed the Lewis and Clark. The level point of high land Lewis had chosen was about 30 feet above the high-tide line, a couple of hundred yards back from the Netul's west bank, and some four miles east of the Pacific Ocean. Huge, tall evergreen trees covered the area. Clark declared that "this is certainly the most eligable Situation for our purposes of any in its neighbourhood."

The day after arriving at this spot, Clark and five men blazed a trail to the roaring Pacific. They searched for game and a convenient place for extracting salt from seawater. While fallen trees, swamps, and rain-swollen creeks hampered their explorations, they did encounter "a large gange of Elk" which they pursued "through bogs which the wate of a man would Shake for ½ an Acre." "It is almost incredeable to assurt," wrote Clark, "the bogs which those animals can pass through." One elk provided the small party a welcome, hearty dinner and a hide for some shelter against the onslaught of yet another rainy night.

CRAIG HARMEL

In early December the explorers selected a site located on high ground on the south side of the Columbia River, on a small river the natives called Netul. Here there was plenty of timber for construction and fires, elk were abundant, huge trees provided protection against ocean gales, and the Columbia was close by.

Captain Lewis and five men searched for an area in which the Clatsop Indians had said elk were plentiful. After having been gone longer than expected, Clark wrote of Lewis: ". . . a 1000 conjectures has crouded into my mind respecting his probable situation & safty."

Unlike the conventional long rifles of Lewis and Clark's era, the Harpers Ferry rifle was short enough to be loaded into a canoe or on horseback, had no decoration, and used interchangeable parts.

The scouting party spent much of the following day with a group of Indians who received Clark and his men with "extrodeannary friendship" and presented them with fish, berries, and roots; entertained them with gambling games; and gave them mats on which to sleep before the fire.

Clark and his party next explored the raging seacoast, where he examined curious shells, watched Indians gathering fish "frequently thrown up on Shore and left by the tide," and learned from an English-speaking native that "Sturgion was verry good." They later visited an Indian village where Clark was asked to shoot a duck. He astonished both himself and the Indians by shooting the head off the bird at about "30 Steps" with his "Small rifle." The weapon Clark was referring to was probably the Harpers Ferry 1803 flintlock, designed especially for the expedition.

Upon returning to the hilltop encampment, they found the others hard at work cutting down trees to build the fort in which they were to spend the winter. Clark sketched a floor plan, calling for a 50-foot-square structure comprised of three connected huts on one side facing four connecting huts on the opposite side and joined at the ends by palisades. A parade ground, measuring 48 by 20 feet, was to occupy the central part of the fort.

As they built their winter quarters many difficulties continued to plague the expedition. Daily journal entries tell of incessant rainfall, with spurts of snow, hail, and violent winds. The cold, damp weather, combined with rotting and inadequate clothing and a poor diet, made a number of the men ill. Nights seemed especially long and sleepless as fleas infested the wet, half-rotten bedding.

In spite of these problems, construction of the log fort proceeded briskly. Trees of all dimensions grew thickly on the hill overlooking the Netul. Clark called them the "streightest & most butifullest logs." No expedition member documented what kinds of trees were used, but it is assumed the weary men selected those closest at hand including a combination of the most common species: Sitka spruce, Douglas fir, western hemlock, and red alder. The expedition's carpenter, Sergeant Gass, praised "a kind of timber" that "can be split 10 feet long and 2 broad, not more than an inch and a half thick." It took only four days to erect the walls. The men obviously needed no extra inducement to work fast; the sooner they could put a roof over their head, the better.

By December 16, the men had roofed over their "Meet house" just in time to hang and smoke the meat from 16 elk. And by December 22, they had completed four cabins. The next day, Lewis and Clark moved into their "unfinished" room. For comfort they purchased three "verry neetly made" mats from visiting Indians. Private Joseph Fields presented the captains with a table, two chairs, and to each "a wide slab hued to write on."

On Christmas Eve the men finally succeeded in completing most of their compound. They named it Fort Clatsop in honor of the Indians who had befriended and helped them. The enlisted men occupied the row of three rooms along the one side. Charbonneau, Sacagawea, and their infant son Pomp resided in the opposite hut nearest the main gate. The adjoining room contained

DAVID MUENCH

". . . this thick heavy timbered pine country added to the constant cloudy weather makes it difficult for even a good woodsman to steer for any considerable distance the course he wishes."

MERIWETHER LEWIS. JANUARY 26TH, 1806

JAMES STOFFER

"∴ . . they imediately all came out and appeared to assume new life, the sight of This Indian woman, [Sacagawea] wife to one of our interpr. [Toussaint Charbonneau] confirmed those people of our friendly intentions, as no woman ever accompanies a war party of Indians in this quarter."

CLARK ON THE COLUMBIA, 1805

15

During the entire journey, music and dance proved to be an excellent means of uplifting the men's morale. In spite of the difficulties experienced on the Pacific coast, the members of the expedition were eager to let themselves be entertained by the fiddle-playing Peter Cruzatte and George Gibson.

the captains' quarters, which boasted the only full fireplace and which, for extra privacy and defense, did not open directly onto the central parade ground. The orderly's room came next, probably occupied by both Clark's servant, York, and the sergeant of the guard. A small meat store-room completed the structure.

On Christmas morning Lewis and Clark "we[re] awoke by the discharge of the fire arm[s] of all our party & a Selute, Shouts and a Song which the whole party joined in under our windows. . . ." Clark wrote that the members "were chearfull all the morning . . ." After breakfast the explorers exchanged gifts. The captains distributed tobacco and silk handkerchiefs; Lewis presented Clark with a "fleece hosrie" (long woolen underwear), shirt draws, and socks; and from others Clark received a pair of moccasins, a small Indian basket, and ermine tails. Christmas dinner consisted of poor elk meat, spoiled pounded

The fiddle was useful for entertainment and diplomacy. Between the expedition and every Indian nation they met, there were the usual differences in customs and languages. But time and again the explorers discovered that they had in common with nearly every Native American tribe a fondness for two things: music and dance.

fish, and a few roots—all "without salt to season," lamented Patrick Gass. Sergeant Ordway declared that even though "we have no ardent Spirits, all are in good health which we esteem more than all the ardent Spirits in the world." Clark noted "in the evening all the party Snugly fixed in their huts."

After Christmas the men put the finishing touches on the fort, erecting stockade fencing and gates and completing chimneys for the badly smoking fireplaces in the squad rooms. Five men were dispatched with "5 of the largest kittles" to boil seawater for the extraction of salt. This party established a camp some 15 miles southwest of Fort Clatsop, within the present-day city of Seaside, Oregon, at a site that provided fresh water, game, firewood, and friendly Indians. A few days later, two of the men returned to report that the party was daily producing from three quarts to a gallon of salt, and they presented a sample that Lewis described as "excellent, fine, strong, & white" and "a great treat."

On the last day of 1805, Clark directed the men to dig "Sinks" for toilets and to erect a "Sentinal Box." With the dawning of 1806, "I was awoke at an early hour," wrote Lewis, "by the discharge of a volley of small arms, which were fired by our party in front of our quarters to usher in the new year." He observed, however, that the day's greatest joy was the anticipation of New Year's Day, 1807, when they would "participate in the mirth and hilarity of the day," enjoying the food of civilization among family and friends.

". . . the four men who had been sent to assist the saltmakers in transporting meat which they had killed to their camp, also returned, and brought with them all the salt which had been made, consisting of about one busshel only. with the means we have of boiling the salt water we find it a very tedious operation, that of making salt, notwithstanding we keep the Kettles boiling day and night. we calculate on three bushels lasting us from hence to our deposits of that article on the Missouri."

MERIWETHER LEWIS. FEBRUARY 3, 1806

When Clark and his party prepared to set out to investigate a beached whale, Sacagawea insisted that she too be allowed to see "the great waters" and "monstrous fish."

Still, he noted they were presently content with eating boiled elk meat, roots, and slaking their thirst with their only beverage, *pure water.*

The salt-making party had also discovered a beached whale and sent back some blubber that Lewis and Clark described as "very pallitable and tender." Clark decided to go "in quest of the whale," taking with him 12 men. But Sacagawea strenuously objected. She observed that "She had traveled a long way with us to See the great waters, and that now that monstrous fish [actually a marine mammal] was also to be Seen, She thought it verry hard that She could not be permitted to See either." Indeed, she had come a very long way with her son on her back, enduring the same countless hardships and hundreds of miles as had the men. The captains relented and she joined the trek to the seashore and its whale.

On their way, the party enjoyed the first fair night in two months. After visiting the salt-makers, they ascended an "emence mountain the top of which was obscured in the clouds." After two hours of climbing an "almost perpindecular" path, they reached the coastal summit of what is now called Tillamook Head, on which the fatigued party camped for the night. In the morning, "from this point," wrote Clark, "I beheld the grandest and most pleasing prospects which my eyes ever surveyed, in my frount a boundless Ocean; to the N. and N.E. the coast . . . as far as my sight could be extended, the Seas rageing with emence wave[s]. . . ." From this thousand-foot peak, Clark observed to the south that the force with which the surf broke against "inoumerable rocks of emence Sise out at a great distance from the shore," gave the Oregon coast "a most romantic appearance." The explorers named this spot "Clark's Point of View."

After 19 months of difficult travel through some 4,000 miles of wilderness, the intrepid explorers finally saw and heard the waves of the Pacific Ocean.

When Clark and his party finally found the beached whale, they discovered that the "Killamox" Indians, also known to be called the Tillamook Indians, had already taken "every Valuable part," leaving only the skeleton of Clark's "Monster," which was possibly a California gray whale. Nearby the natives were boiling blubber in large wooden troughs. The animal's bladder and intestines provided containers for the oil, which the Indians bartered with "great reluctiance and in small quantities only." With "utmost exertion" Clark succeeded in purchasing a few gallons of oil and three hundred pounds of blubber. "Small as this stock is," Clark wrote, "I prise it highly; and thank providence for directing the whale to us; and think him much more kind to us than he

was to jonah, having Sent this Monster to be *Swallowed by us* in Sted of *Swallowing of us* as jonah's did."

News of newly completed Fort Clatsop quickly spread among the surrounding Indian tribes. Lewis and Clark were well aware that their small party was vastly outnumbered by the native populations. Consequently, they instituted strict rules to help avoid trouble and secure the explorers' safety. For example, they insisted that the men must treat the natives fairly as well as firmly and must not strike or assault an Indian unless in self-defense. All enlisted men except cooks and interpreters were to take turns in 24-hour guard detail. At all times a sentinel was to be stationed in front of the commanding officers' quarters. Privates were to announce the arrival of Indian parties. At sunset, Charbonneau, a sergeant, and two privates were to clear all visiting Indians from the compound, and the main gate was to be locked until sunrise. Special rules were implemented to safeguard tools, weapons, ammunition, and the meathouse key, and the men were to make certain their canoes were well secured down at the river.

While almost continuous rainfall, illness, and flea-infested rooms continued to plague the explorers, the party remained industrious. A tremendous amount of time and effort was required to maintain an adequate food supply. Fortunately, the men's hunting skills matched their prodigious appetites. Hunters left the fort nearly every day, while others hauled heavy loads of elk meat and hides back to the compound. Soon, Lewis wrote, the men were "very much engaged in dressing Elk and Deer skins for mockersons and cloathing." Half-rotten meat was dried or jerked to make it more palatable.

Lewis's "Air-gun" fired a lethal lead shot with air compressed into the hollow, cylindrical stock.

The large number of elk taken by the hunters provided ample skins to replace rotting buckskins. But considerable work remained to "dress" (tan) the hides and sew them into clothing. Just 78 days after arriving at Fort Clatsop, Captain Lewis reported "the men have provided themselves very amply with mockersons and leather cloathing, much more so indeed than they ever have since they have been on this voige."

Elk were first introduced to science by Meriwether Lewis at Fort Clatsop, and were chiefly responsible for the expedition's decision to remain encamped on the coast during the winter of 1805-06. Known today as "Roosevelt elk," they provided tons of meat for food and enough skins to make new clothing for the entire party. For the members it was "unwelcom information and reather alarming" to learn that the elk had gone from their usual hunting grounds back into the mountains, far from Fort Clatsop. This, in part, contributed to the expeditions's departure earlier than originally planned.

CRAIG HARMEL

The most skilled of hunters, George Droulliard, a nonmilitary member of the expedition, was admired not only by Captain Lewis, who wrote that "I scarcely know how we should subsist were it not for the exertions of this excellent hunter," but by the Indians as well. After watching Droulliard shoot several elk, the natives were amazed by both the explorer's marksmanship and the excellence of his rifle. Lewis and Clark believed, in fact, that the Indians' respect for their shooting skills and their firearms would likely deter "any acts of hostility if they have ever meditated any such." Lewis's "Air-gun" also astonished the Indians. This Austrian-style weapon had been brought along in the event the expedition ran out of black powder. When fully charged, it could shoot several lead shot without powder or loud noise. The natives could not understand such force and therefore concluded that it was "*great medicine* which comprehends every thing that is to them incomprehensible."

By contrast, the Indians generally had little success in hunting game. The explorers shot many elk that had only been wounded by arrows. The Indians achieved occasional success by constructing deep pits behind fallen trees, into which "the unwary Elk in passing the tree precipitates himself into the pitt" and was thus captured.

Other than elk herds, wildlife was scarce. Bears were hibernating, deer were rarely encountered, and beavers and other small mammals were hard to find. Clark wrote that the numerous ducks and other waterfowl were extremely wary "owing to their being much hunted and pursued by the Indians in their Canoes." As winter progressed, the hunters were forced to travel farther and farther from the fort to locate elk, and the meat packers had to carry their heavy loads as far as nine miles through densely forested and soggy terrain.

The damp climate, with temperatures generally above freezing, caused much of the meat to spoil by the time it reached the fort. Such tainted meat, described as "poor and inferior," became their "principle dependance for subsistence." The cooks did the best they could to vary the recipes of this generally monotonous diet, and Lewis once commented on "an excellent supper" of marrowbone and a brisket of boiled elk that had "the appearance of a little fat on it. This for Fort Clatsop is living in high stile [*sic*]."

Throughout the winter, the Clatsop's Chief Coboway and his people often traded or brought gifts of such native foods as fish, whale blubber, roots, berries, and other wild fruits. Lewis discovered that an edible thistle, which the natives called "Shannetahque," was "crisp as a carrot." Horsetail or "rush" was "reather insipid in point of flavour." The "most Valuable" of all roots, the "Wappetoe," tasted like a potato.

At one particularly discouraging time when the diet was so poor that a number of sick men were not recovering their strength, relief came when Droulliard, who had been trading with the

21

CRAIG HARMEL

STEVE HENRIKSON

The expedition learned from the Clatsop and Chinook Indians that Wappato roots were good to eat. Captain Clark noted, "those roots are equal to the Irish potato, and is a tolerable substitute for bread."

WILLIAM CLARK. NOVEMBER 22, 1805

From the Clatsops, Lewis and Clark purchased several conical hats made of cedar bark and beargrass. Lewis noted they were ". . . wrought with the fingers so closely . . ." that they were "nearly waterproof." As a man walked in the rain, swinging fringe attached to buckskin clothing would cast off drops of water.

Clatsops, returned "with a most acceptable supply of fat Sturgeon, fresh Anchovies and . . . a bushel of Wappetoe." The exhuberant Lewis described these welcome provisions as a feast.

In March, when millions of eulachon were running up the rivers to spawn, Chief Coboway brought a supply that Lewis found "superior to any fish I ever tasted." This member of the smelt family was so oily that Northwest Indians would draw a wick through a dried one in order to use it as a candle; thus the name candlefish.

The men were also kept busy making elk hides into clothing. By January 18, Lewis observed that they were already "much engaged in dressing skins in order to cloath themselves . . . for our homeward journey." The men's main difficulty, as explained by Lewis, was their "want of branes"; Lewis was not referring to his men's intelligence but rather to the key ingredient in the frontier tanning process: animal brains. The process, described in Sergeant Gass's journal as a "laborious business," was simple enough but fatiguing. They first scraped off the hair and flesh. Next the brains of the animals were worked deep into the skin.

This was followed by several tedious hours of stretching and rubbing until the skin became permanently soft and ready to be sewn into clothing.

Accustomed to near-total outdoor living, these men attached dangling fringe to their buckskin shirts and pants for a purpose other than decoration. Raindrops ran down to the tips of the swinging fringe, which would twist and whip with every movement a man would make, thereby casting droplets off the clothing. The resulting tough leather garb served the explorers well, protecting them against brambles and other thorny shrubs while providing insulation from the cold and keeping them dry during moderate rain showers.

Other animal hides were occasionally used, such as a coat of the "Tiger Cat" that the Indians made for Captain Lewis; and a "westcoat" that Clark made from the pelts of the sea otter, a marine mammal found abundantly in the sea along the coast.

The captains completed their wardrobe by asking some Clatsop women to weave for them custom-fitted conical, brimless hats that were so

Salal: "the fruit is a deep perple berry about the size of buck short [sic] or common black cherry. . . ."

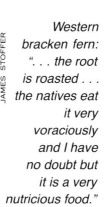

In writing about the trees of the Pacific Northwest, Lewis modestly remarked, ". . . I shall discribe as well as my slender botanicall skil wil enable me . . ." But in spite of his humble self-evaluation, Lewis's observations demonstrate a very respectable ability.

Western bracken fern: ". . . the root is roasted . . . the natives eat it very voraciously and I have no doubt but it is a very nutricious food."

tightly woven as to effectively shed raindrops. The Indian women presented the captains with "excellent hats made of Cedar bark and ornamented with beargrass." Several more were purchased and distributed among the party.

During the winter at Fort Clatsop, Lewis devoted hours upon hours to observing and writing about the flora and fauna, the geography, and other aspects of the natural environment. Contrasting with Clark's terse, forthright prose, Lewis composed detailed, penetrating, and sometimes moving entries. His numerous observations and discoveries were, in fact, among the expedition's very most important achievements. So precise were his descriptions and his use of many technical botanical terms that botanists subsequently had no difficulty identifying his discoveries. He described some three dozen plant species from the surrounding region, ten of which were then new to science. He also recorded important ecological, geographical, and economic information about each new species and displayed as well his skill as an ethnobotanist by carefully describing how the Indians used various plants for food, clothing, and tools.

In describing the leaf of the grand fir, Lewis demonstrated his ability to delineate important features of a plant: "it's leaves are sessile, acerose, one ⅛ of an inch in length and ⅙th of an inch in width, . . . gibbous, a little declining, obtusely pointed, soft flexible, and the upper disk longitudinally marked with a slight channel."

But in addition to his thorough botanical descriptions, Lewis's writing reflected more than a

Overleaf: As the months rolled by, thoughts turned to home—4,000 river miles away. Photo by David Muench.

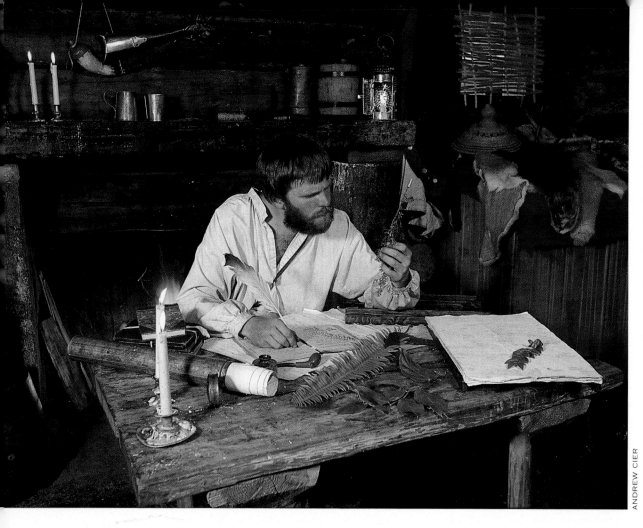

Meriwether Lewis described and collected numerous plants at Fort Clatsop. Some were simply mentioned in passing, while others were described in elaborate botanical detail. Many of the specimens Lewis collected on the Pacific coast are still preserved at the Academy of Natural Sciences of Philadelphia.

ANDREW CIER

scientific curiosity about the new plants he discovered. For him, seashore lupine possessed a root of "disagreeable bitterness," while edible thistle, called "Shannetahque" by the natives, had a sweet root "precisely that of the sugar in flavor." The wood of the Oregon crab apple tree was "excessively hard when seasoned" and provided useful "ax handles as well as glutts or wedges" for the explorers. And western bracken, a species of fern that "produces no flower or fruit whatever," still merited a compliment as a "beautifull plant" in the eyes of Lewis.

Tremendously huge conifers inhabiting the environs near Fort Clatsop impressed Lewis. The Sitka spruce, he wrote, "grows to immence size; very commonly 27 feet in the girth six feet above the surface of the earth, and in several instances we have found them as much as 36 feet in the girth or 12 feet diameter perfectly solid and entire. they frequently rise to the hight of 230 feet, and one hundred and twenty or 30 of that hight without a limb." Western hemlock was "next in dignity in point of size. . . . much the most common species" and in Lewis's estimation constituted "at least one half of the timber in this neighbourhood."

Lewis provided ethnobotanical information with more than half the plants he referred to

When Captain Lewis referred to the "arbor-vita" [arborvitae], which means "tree of life," he was referring to the western red cedar. This light, durable, and easy-to-split wood was observed by Lewis to be the principal raw material for construction in the Chinookan culture.

ANDREW CIER

"The hunters who were over the Netull the other day informed us that they measured a pine tree, (or fir No. 1) [Sitka spruce] which at the hight of a man's breast was 42 feet in the girth; about three feet higher, or as high as a tall man could reach, it was 40 feet in the girth which was about the circumpherence for at least 200 feet without a limb. . . . It had every appearance of being perfectly sound."

Meriwether Lewis.
Monday, March 10th 1806

ANDREW CIER

while at Fort Clatsop. "The native roots," he commented, "furnish a considerable proportion of the subsistence of the indians." The root of the "rush" or horsetail, was "most used by the Killamucks" on the coast. Natives closer to Fort Clatsop "eat the root of the Cattail or Cooper's flag," which to Lewis was "pleasantly taisted." But the root most revered by all coastal Indians, wappato, grew a considerable distance away "in the marshey grounds of the beatiful and firtile valley on the Columbia." Wappato thus became "a principal article of traffic [trade] between the inhabitants of the valley and those of . . . [the] coast."

The fruit of local plants was also a favorite among local tribes. The small, deep purple berry of the evergreen huckleberry was eaten either ripe off the bush or "dried in the sun for winter uce." Huge amounts of salal berries would be pounded

and then baked in 10- or 15-pound loaves in "sw[e]ating kilns." The resulting "bread" would be broken and stirred in cold water "untill it be sufficiently thick and then eaten." And the bear-berry produced what Lewis considered a "very tasteless and insippid fruit." However, its dried, crumpled leaves served as a suitable substitute for the expedition's depleted tobacco supply.

Lewis's frequent references to western red cedar illustrated this tree's unique importance to the Chinookan culture. It was used for constructing nearly every item in the coastal Indian household as well as 50-foot-long canoes and parts of weapons such as bows and arrows. Domestic utensils such as bowls, platters, and spoons were carved out of cedar. From cedar bark they wove mats, bags, and baskets and made their nets and fishing lines. A principal raw material for build-

ROBERT C. FIELDS—ANIMALS ANIMALS

North America's most common swan was named by Lewis "from the peculiar whistleing of the note of this bird I have called it the whistleing swan. . . . we first saw them below the great narrows of the Columbia near the Chilluckkittequaw nation. They are very abundant in this neighbourhood and have remained with us all winter."

MERIWETHER LEWIS. MARCH 9TH. 1806

JOHN GERLACK—ANIMALS ANIMALS

With a 300-word plus description, Lewis formally introduced the ring-necked duck to science. Among its many features, he noted, "the beak of this duck is remarkably wide, and is 2 inches in length. . . ."

LYNN M. STONE—ANIMALS ANIMALS

ing houses was the easy-to-split, durable cedar. Shredded cedar bark, "interwoven in the middle by means of several cords of the same materials," created a "tissue" from which clothes would be made. And cedar fibers woven into cord bound infants to cradle boards and burial mats around canoes.

Lewis's descriptions of a hundred or more animals indigenous to the lower Columbia River re-

gion were even more impressive. Dozens of them were then new to science, and all, at greater or lesser length, received the same meticulous attention as did the plants. And, in addition to providing detailed information on anatomy, habits, and geographical range, Lewis included native uses and economic importance.

Inasmuch as Lewis was a skillful pioneering naturalist, little if anything escaped his vision in

28

MICKEY GIBSON—ANIMALS ANIMALS

Lewis was impressed by the beauty of the Douglas squirrel and recorded that "the throat, breast, belley and inner part of the legs are of a pale brick red."

DAVID C. FRITTS—ANIMALS ANIMALS

Another bird first described by Lewis and Clark was the western grebe, which ". . . dives for security when pursued."

Mountain beaver.

LEONARD LEE RUE III—ANIMALS ANIMALS

the surrounding virgin wilderness. In his opinion the "tyger Cat," now known as the Oregon bobcat, was "much the same in form, agility and ferosity" as those in the East. The "Pole-cat," better known today as the striped skunk, was "very abundant on some parts of the columbia . . . and feed on the offal of the Indian fishing shores." His observation that the western badger ate "flesh, roots, bugs, and wild fruits" suggested that he examined stomach contents. And his declaration that the Douglas squirrel, or chickaree, was "a beautifull little animal" showed again that he had more than a scientific curiosity about nature. Other lower Columbia mammals of which Lewis gave the first formal description were Roosevelt elk, mountain beaver, Townsend's chipmunk, western gray squirrel, Townsend's mole and Richardson's red squirrel.

Varieties of marine life abounded in the nearby Pacific and the Columbia River, and Lewis described many in earnest. In the course of his writings he referred to marine mammals, shellfish, amphibians, and fish characteristic of the Northwest. But no marine animal attracted his attention more than the sea otter, which provided "the most esteemed and valuable of . . . robes . . ." Lewis considered its pelt as "the riches[t] and I think the most delicious fur in the world at least I cannot form an idea of any more so."

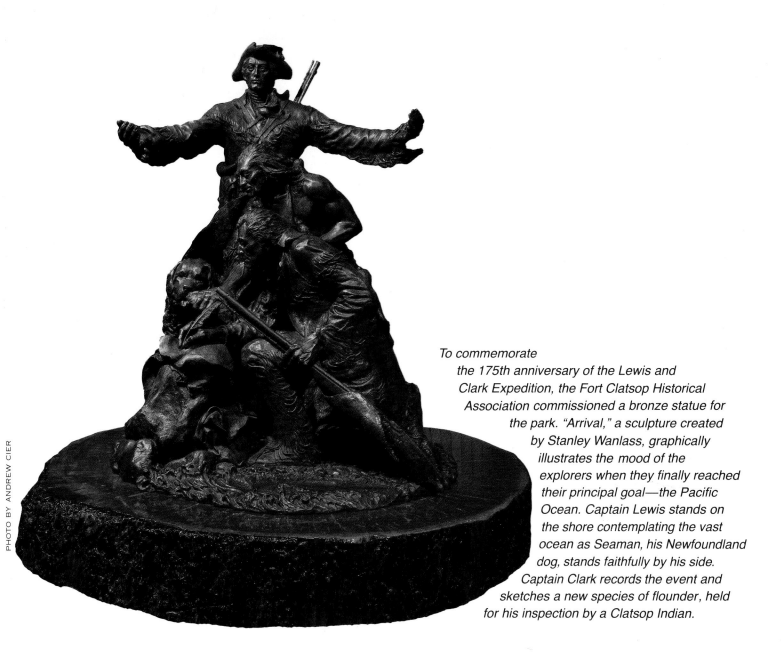

To commemorate the 175th anniversary of the Lewis and Clark Expedition, the Fort Clatsop Historical Association commissioned a bronze statue for the park. "Arrival," a sculpture created by Stanley Wanlass, graphically illustrates the mood of the explorers when they finally reached their principal goal—the Pacific Ocean. Captain Lewis stands on the shore contemplating the vast ocean as Seaman, his Newfoundland dog, stands faithfully by his side. Captain Clark records the event and sketches a new species of flounder, held for his inspection by a Clatsop Indian.

visability of establishing Fort Clatsop as a national monument.

The National Park Service next conducted an archaeological field study of the site. No evidence was found, but the results were not surprising considering the expedition's circumstances. Historians point out that the Corps of Discovery had traveled some 4,000 miles by foot, horseback, and canoe to reach the Pacific. Certainly any item carried that far would be too important to leave behind.

Shortly afterward the National Park Service received its most convincing evidence concerning Fort Clatsop's original location. In 1957, 87-year-old Harlan C. Smith provided oral testimony of his recollections of 1872–80 when he had lived on the site. Mr. Smith was the great-nephew of Carlos Shane, who had burned the original fort logs he had discovered on his land claim in 1850.

Smith explained that a single partially burned log from the original fort had managed to survive into the 1870s and that members of his family had passed this information down to him. Smith contributed additional valuable evidence about the original site which the National Park Service considered convincing.

Although there were no archaeological discoveries, Harlan Smith's testimony, together with William Clark's maps and other historical accounts, convinced historians that the Fort Clatsop replica was built on or very near the original site. On May 29, 1958, President Dwight D. Eisenhower signed a bill establishing Fort Clatsop National Memorial. The fort had played a significant role in the success of the Lewis and Clark Expedition and in shaping the United States. It now became nationally recognized and incorporated into the National Park System.

Fort Clatsop Today

Congress established Fort Clatsop National Memorial "for the purpose of commemorating the culmination, and winter encampment, of the Lewis and Clark Expedition following its successful crossing of the North American continent." Charged with this mission, the park's interpretive program explains the historical significance of Lewis and Clark's epic journey; the important contribution that Native Americans made to the success of the expedition; what daily life was like at Fort Clatsop; and the courage, fortitude, and problem-solving abilities displayed by the men of the expedition.

Visitors to this 125-acre memorial are first welcomed to a visitor center where museum displays and audiovisual programs tell about the famed exploration of the Corps of Discovery. "Arrival," a heroic-size bronze statue of Lewis and Clark and a Clatsop Indian, commands a strong presence in the building's lobby. Created by Stanley Wanlass on the occasion of Fort Clatsop's 175th anniversary, the statue is symbolic of the exhilaration and amazement felt by the explorers as they first viewed the Pacific Ocean.

The replica and original site of Fort Clatsop are obscured from view from the visitor center. As visitors leave the building they journey forth on a miniexploration of their own along a path that leads from the twentieth century back into the past. A short walk brings them to the restoration area. With signs of modern civilization absent, a visitor standing at the gates to Fort Clatsop has an ideal spot from which to imagine the presence of the expedition. Huge coniferous trees, similar to those that so impressed Meriwether Lewis, stand guard over the site. A steep slope to the southeast leads to a view of the Lewis and Clark River, which was the explorers' link with the Columbia River and home. Rising high beyond the river is Saddle Mountain, a basalt prominence and a point of reference for the expedition's hunters. Rough terrain with almost impenetrable vegetation, against which Fort Clatsop provided a humble but satisfactory respite, is visible in all directions.

The Fort Clatsop replica was expertly built by local Finnish carpenters over a period of a year and probably looks more refined than the original fort erected in a mere 15 days by the wet and weary explorers. Yet it is a faithful reproduction, based upon the same floor plans and dimensions as laid down by William Clark. Visitors cannot help but feel they are walking in Lewis and Clark's

"Living history" demonstrations at the fort give visitors insight into daily life there in 1805–06. Guests are invited to witness or participate in the explorers' methods of survival while they hear about the numerous hardships endured throughout the journey. Included in the various hands-on experiences is the chance to sew elk skin moccasins or smell the unmistakable fragrance of fresh-cut cedar as it becomes a new roof. No better appreciation of the explorers' skills can be gained than by those who attempt to ignite a flint-and-steel fire in the rain. Visitors are invited to try.

moccasins as they enter the fort's parade ground.

Fort Clatsop today may best be described as a "living museum" where, during the summer months, interpreters recreate some of the activities of the 1805–06 winter encampment. Visitors are often invited to participate in these activities.

The atmosphere at the fort is intended to help visitors experience some of the same feelings and perceptions as those of the expedition. The powerful report of black-powder weapons periodically cracks through the air while sounds of wood chopping, hide scraping, and fiddle music may also be heard. Smoke from alder and cedar fires creates a pleasing fragrance as elk meat and salmon are smoked and cured. Rooms are dimly lit by tallow candles, and feet must steady themselves on uneven floors. Hands find pleasure in feeling the soft, smooth furs of beaver and otter. The captains' quarters are filled with faithfully reproduced replicas of original journals, maps, drawings, plant collections, and Indian artifacts.

Interpretive talks and demonstrations offer insights into the abilities of the explorers. Park rangers portray themselves as proficient nineteenth-century wilderness survivors. In seconds they start fires with flint and steel. They are familiar with the hours of tedium required to dress an animal skin and sew it into a buckskin uniform,

JAMES STOFFER

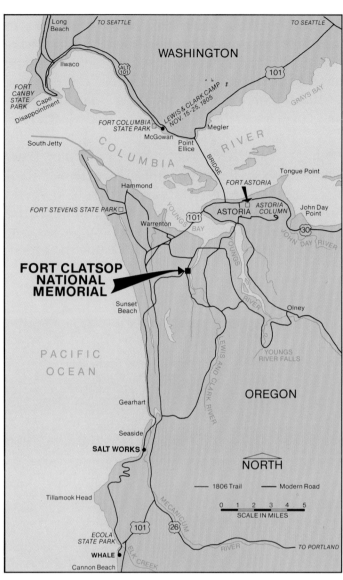

and they demonstrate five ways to make it water repellent. They create tools from bone and wood, cast lead shot, keep a razor-sharp edge on their knives, make elk skin rope, and illustrate the operation of the flintlock rifle with black-powder demonstrations. To provide lighting for the fort's dark rooms, huge amounts of animal fat are rendered into tallow for the purpose of making candles. Wood is chopped and hauled for fires. Elk and deer meat are cut and hung to be smoked.

But more than just the task of demonstrating survival takes place at Fort Clatsop. Interpreters invite guests to follow them on "discovery walks" and observe some of the very plant species introduced to science by Meriwether Lewis. Visitors may have the chance to taste wild berries on an ethnobotany walk. On such excursions interpreters explain, as did Lewis, how the many plants provided the local natives with food, clothing, tools, and materials with which to build their homes. A plant press, similar to the one Lewis used to preserve botanical specimens for President Jefferson, is also demonstrated.

A short path leads north from the fort to a spring believed to have supplied water to the expedition. This raging torrent, with a cascading waterfall during the winter months, is reduced to a mere trickle in the summer.

SUGGESTED READING

ALLEN, JOHN LOGAN. *Lewis and Clark and the Image of the American Northwest.* New York: Dover Publications, 1991.

AMBROSE, STEPHEN E. *Undaunted Courage.* New York: Simon & Schuster, 1996.

BAKELESS, JOHN. *Lewis and Clark: Partners in Discovery.* New York: Dover Publications, 1996.

COUES, ELLIOTT, ed. *The History of the Lewis and Clark Expedition: By Meriwether Lewis and William Clark.* New York: Dover Publications, 1893.

CUTRIGHT, PAUL RUSSELL. *Lewis and Clark: Pioneering Naturalists.* Lincoln: University of Nebraska Press, 1989.

DEVOTO, BERNARD, ed. *The Journals of Lewis and Clark.* Boston: Houghton Mifflin Company, 1953.

MOULTON, GARY, ed. *The Journals of the Lewis and Clark Expedition.* Lincoln: University of Nebraska Press, 1983-2000 (13 volumes).

MURPHY, DAN. *Lewis and Clark: Voyage of Discovery.* Las Vegas, Nevada: KC Publications, 1977.

Another trail leads down from the fort to the place on the Lewis and Clark River where the explorers landed their canoes on December 7, 1805. Restoration of this site is proceeding; one goal is to have five large dugout canoes there, as did the expedition. The interpreters occasionally navigate the first two of these 35-foot canoes on the river. Virtually unnavigable with fewer than five paddlers per canoe, the interpreters quickly learn how very capable were the expedition's "boatmen," for even on this relatively calm stretch of water, these cumbersome craft are difficult to maneuver.

The interpretive staff at Fort Clatsop spend hours perfecting their skills and gaining experiences relating to the expedition and its participants. These activities include tasting their food, using their weapons, wearing their clothes, and sleeping in their fort, to name but a few. The aim is to equip them with real life experiences so they can better answer visitors' questions about what life must have been like long ago.

The disagreeable experiences of the expedition on their unprecedented journey remind us that our nation's strength and growth were achieved through hardship and sacrifice. In each program or demonstration, the interpreter illustrates how the explorers used their fortitude and problem-solving talents to cope courageously with the wilderness. Fort Clatsop National Memorial's ultimate goal is to inspire visitors to apply those same qualities to meet today's challenges.

NPS PHOTO BY TOM GRAY

"we . . . shal set out as soon as the weather will permit."
MERIWETHER LEWIS, MARCH 17TH. 1806

Inside back cover: A park interprete experiences the night Fort Clatsop National Memoria NPS Photo by Sal Castr

Back cover: A cultural demonstrat of Shoshone descent portra Sacagawea. Photo by Craig Harme

Created, Designed, and Published in the U.S..
Ink formulated by Daihan Ink Co., Lt
Printing by Doosan Corporation, Seoul, Kore
Paper produced exclusively by Hankuk Paper Mfg. Co., Lt